32 DAYS:
MY
HOMELESS
EXPERIENCE

YOULANDA O. WILLIAMS

ISBN 978-1-0980-9374-7 (paperback)
ISBN 978-1-0980-9375-4 (digital)

Christian Faith Publishing, Inc.
832 Park Avenue
Meadville, PA 16335
www.christianfaithpublishing.com

Printed in the United States of America

I t was March 13, 2020, at 6:00 p.m. and my birthday, when I went to urgent care because my throat and ear were hurting. I was told to go to the other side of the hospital due to the COVID-19 pandemic, which individuals were referred to for possible coronavirus infection. Well, thank God, it was just an ear infection, and my throat was sore due to the postnasal drip. This was the beginning of my thirty-two days of homelessness experience.

I was living with a male friend whom I've known for sixteen years because I gave up my apartment of three years because I couldn't afford the new rent hike. California rent was skyrocketing, and many people couldn't afford the rent hikes. In Long Beach, there was no rent control, and the landlords could raise the rent over 10 percent if they provide a sixty-day notice, and if the rent control bill passed they would get the max if there was going to be rent control. The city was trying to get rent control in Long Beach, California, so the landlords raised their rent. My rent went from $1,250 to $1,365, and I was barely able to pay the $1,250, being I only worked thirty hours a week. So when I received the notice, I knew I had to do something. I had excellent credit, but I didn't have the down payment to move into another unit, so I was thankful to have my friend I thought, to let me stay with him. This was the precursor of the story.

After leaving the urgent care, I went to my other friend's house, someone I liked and thought would never hurt me, but he did. However, I received a text from him saying, "OMW" (on my way), and that was odd because he had previously told me he wouldn't be able to see me for my birthday because he had something to do that evening and wanted to take me out the day before. I said, "No, thanks." After getting out of urgent care and getting my medicine,

I drove to his house because he didn't answer his phone, and that wasn't like him. *Why, why did I do that?* Well, I guess that's a woman's intuition, and it's a strong force.

I believe it was also the Holy Spirit because I truly believe this man was a good man, and I thought highly of him, and like I said before, he would never hurt me. But God said put *no man* before him. My intuition was right, and the Holy Spirit kept me calm because he was there in his house with another woman and her little kid. I didn't believe my eyes, so I blinked several times, hoping it wasn't what I was seeing, but unfortunately it was. My heart sank. The man who I believed was so true, loving, nurturing, caring, and encouraging betrayed me. When I was inside urgent care, he had left a message and said he wanted to stop by to give me something for my birthday. This was after he lied about not seeing me for my birthday. It all came out and he was not seeing me because he had her at his place.

You don't know, I truly believed I had found a *good* man! I know I wasn't having sex, but I really believed he would have told me the truth if he was seeing someone else because I believe we had that type of relationship. God lets you know if you're willing to listen, and that one needs to put their true *trust in Him*. With tears in my eyes and driving on the 105 freeway to get home without getting to an accident, I was crushed. It was about 10:30 p.m. I walked into my friend's house where I was living, and he told me he wanted to talk to me.

We had not really been speaking for about two weeks, and I had been at his house since November. During this time, he really made me feel as if he really didn't want me to live with him, but since I helped him in 2013, when he lost his job and had to move out of his place, I guess he felt he had to repay the favor. Nevertheless, he began to tell me that the manager had asked him again about how long I was going to stay with him because I was not supposed to be on any of the properties they own. I had sued them prior and won my case regarding an iron door that I placed on my apartment in which they thought they weren't going to pay for and keep it on their property. Well the conversation didn't go well at all. Plus, I didn't totally believe

4

him because of his attitude for the last two weeks about what, I don't know and I didn't care.

I'm never there, and I try to stay out the house until 9:00 p.m. and then come in and go to sleep. That's a pretty hard thing to do, be out the house at 11:00 a.m. to 9:00 p.m. I would sit in my car for hours and watch movies on my phone or talk to someone on the phone. Anyway, he said things to me that I thought he would never say, and I said things to him too. He said he needed me out the house by the twenty-eighth because he was going back to his country for a couple of weeks. I said, "No, I can leave tonight." And after getting all my stuff and five trips up and down the stairs, it was 12:30 a.m. I was *literally* homeless, living in my car!

I went to talk to my friend who leaves in an RV in Long Beach and I told him what happened. He couldn't believe it. He offered and said I can stay with him, but I wasn't going to live in his run-down motor home; even then I had standards. Wow, LOL. I asked him to help me move my stuff from the other guy's apartment to the storage I had, and he said yes he would help me. I left him and went where I used to live, which I felt was familiar territory, I said my prayers, put the seat back, and feel asleep.

THE FIRST MORNING

Waking up to people walking by the car and having such a feeling of shame was…well, I can't put it in words, but it was a feeling I never had in my entire life. However, I said my prayers again, thanking God for protecting me and waking me up. It meant a lot to say that, as I've said that same prayer before, but it truly has meaning this time. This was a feeling I had to get over quick because this is what it is: *you're homeless and living in your car.* I called my friend who lives in the RV, and he helped me get the rest of my things from the other guy's apartment and took them to storage. We had lunch and talked for a while. It was getting dark, and I said, "Well, I'll go find somewhere to sleep." He asked me again if I wanted to stay with him in his motor home; I said no again because it was worse than sleeping in my car.

I found a place to sleep and quickly realized that the homeless community has a way of using nonverbal communication to let you know that, "this is my spot, find your own spot." This black guy gave me such a dirty look that I knew I had to find another place to park my car.

KEEPING CLEAN

I had to go to McDonald's to clean up. I have to give props to McDonald's on South and Cherry in Long Beach. They are the only fast food place that kept their doors open during the pandemic and gave their customers use of the restrooms. It angered me to know that the restaurants didn't let the public use the restroom but took their money. I stop going to the McDonald's on Del Amo Blvd. and Long Beach Blvd. who had the nerve to put a sign on the door that said Out of Service.

CALLING THE CONSTRUCTION FRIEND

It was March 17, 2020, and I had been in my car for four days. I had a meeting with the EEOC over the phone, and my charger was slowing charging my phone. I was worried that my phone would cut off in the meeting, so I called another friend. I don't want to give names in my story because they know who they are, but I want to keep their names anonymous. I didn't want to call him because he really wasn't for me. He was playing games, and I hadn't talked with him in several months. Nevertheless, I needed to charge my phone and I couldn't go anywhere to charge it. Everything was closed down, libraries, restaurants, and workplace centers, due to the COVID-19 pandemic.

He was willing to help, but I believe it was because he hadn't talked to me in a while and wanted to know what I had been up to. It was so hard to tell him what my friend of sixteen years did and the other guy did whom I respected so much. He was jealous of the other guy because I used to talk about how good this guy was and understanding, blah, blah, and blah. Now, I had to say he was just like the rest of the men out here, straight liars.

I will call this friend construction man so I can have some distinction between "friends." He tells me he will get me a room where he is because he can't see me living in my car. The Holy Spirit said, "Don't believe him. He's lying." Therefore, I didn't take it to heart and said okay, but I knew he wasn't going to. He called me the next night while he was at work. He works at night and had the nerve to ask me, what I was doing. I said, "I'm in my car about to get some sleep because it's pretty cold." He wanted to hold a long conversation as if I was in my apartment so he can pass his time at work. He had no clue that I was nervous and scared, and it was traumatic for me because I had never been through this before.

Finally, I told him, "I'm going to sleep now." Before we get off the phone, he said, "Be safe." It took a lot of strength not to curse him out, but the Holy Spirit helped me. He didn't call me for three days, and when he did, he said he had some issues with some employees fighting on the job. I didn't believe him because employees fighting on the job doesn't last three days. As we talked, I said when a person doesn't keep their word, that's on them, but if they promise and they don't come through, then they really didn't want to do what they promised, and that's pretty messed up.

I haven't talked to him since then, and I don't know if he's sick or just not calling. He could be ill with COVID-19, but I'm not sure. My gut is telling me he's just not calling because he doesn't care about me, and never did. This was such a wake-up call because men will tell you anything to be with you sexually, but it showed me who really had my back, and that was God.

MY FATHER CALLS

My father called me on March 18, 2020. He asked me, "What are you doing?" I told him I'm living in my car and what happened living with my supposed-to-be friend of sixteen years. He said, "Well, we can't have you living in your car, so try to find place (hotel), and let me know." It hurt for a moment because he didn't tell me to come to his house. My father always told me, "Wherever I have a home, you have a home," but I could see that was a lie, and coming from him, it hurt since I truly wanted to believe those words. That's when I knew, words don't mean anything when it comes from people, but if you believe in God's word, believe with all your heart and work toward it, his words will come true for you.

I had never been in this predicament before. I have always had my own place, and I left home at seventeen and never asked my father for help. With all that said, I was still grateful that he came through and paid for five days in a hotel in Carson. I thanked God that my father was still here to help me. What happened to the different men who were supposed to like me? Well, it showed me again that they weren't around because I was not putting out. I chose to keep from sin and not be of this world and have sex, so I stayed in my car and didn't call any guy. I'm glad that I have God in my life to give me strength with that desire because it shows me that men are just in their flesh and not the spirit.

FIVE DAYS IN HOTEL

As I stayed in the hotel, the couple next door was making so much noise having sex. I couldn't sleep. They had sex at least three times from 1:00 a.m. until they left at 11:00 a.m. I had to start singing my worship songs to drown them out. I believe that made them leave or at least realize, that they were sinning.

During my five days at the hotel, I was able to shower, do my hair, and work on my Request for Admission against the school district I was fighting. I still had to handle my legal matters, but I prayed before I started, and I was able to get a lot done. On March 24, I checked out, and I felt nervous because I didn't know where I was going or to park my car. I decided to go back to the area where I felt somewhat safe on Linden Avenue in Long Beach. It was raining pretty bad, but with the rain, I felt a little safer because most people stayed in the house. I sat in the car and watched a movie on my phone. I thought to myself, *This is your home for now and only temporary, and God has you in His hands.* I felt such a peace come over me that it's hard to explain. I would always say my prayers before going to sleep and ask God to protect me while I'm asleep, this was more important now than ever because I was living on the street.

I would wake up and thank God for another day and ask him to help me get through another day. I would go to the McDonald's on Del Amo and Long Beach Boulevard and clean up and brush my teeth. I would buy a breakfast burrito and a small sweet tea so it wouldn't look like I'm homeless. The pride was still there, and even doing this, I still felt as if they *knew* I was homeless. In addition, God has a way of humbling you, and boy was I humbled by this experience.

Even though I get angry about being kicked out in the street by my friend, I quickly asked for forgiveness for my anger. God has forgiven me, and I'm able to move on. I would go and talk to Ms. Joanna, who is a seventy-two-year-old Belizean woman whose former occupation was a LVN. She has been homeless for about twenty-two years. I don't know why she's been out here so long, but it's not for me to question that. I'm here to be used by God and talk with her as she talks and encourages me during this time.

When I started to cry, and I did it often, I would ask God why am I going through this? Then I would think of Ms. Joanna. She praises God even though she doesn't have a car to shelter her from the rain or the cold weather, and she's much older than me. Therefore, I said to myself, *If she can endure with God's help, surely I can continue to endure with His help too.*

One day, I was talking to Ms. Joanna, and I realized that she needed to get another immigration card. I called to the immigration department, and we spoke to a representative named Heather. She was very helpful and gave us the information she needed to get another card. I was trying to finish my Request for Admissions regarding my legal matter against the school district, and my battery was going low on my computer. I needed a car charger and went to Walmart, and they didn't sell them. I was told to buy it from Best Buy. I knew the devil was trying to stop me from finishing my Request for Admissions, but I contacted Best Buy, and they only had one left that was in Downey, and I could pick it up in an hour. I looked up and said, "Thank you, Lord." Some people may say that's luck, but I know it was God, looking out for me and Ms. Joanna. Ms. Joanna needed these papers, and God used me to get them to her. She was so grateful to receive them, and I felt a sense of accomplishment that I was able to help her. We prayed together as we normally did before I would leave to find myself a spot to park my car and go to sleep.

PAYCHECK SHORT ONCE AGAIN FROM SCHOOL DISTRICT

I get paid on the twenty-fifth of March, and I believe I will receive two full weeks of pay. When I received my pay, it's only $529. I was so angry that I contacted the payroll department right away. They said they would give me the balance owed to me on the next check, which would be on April 10, 2020. I was hotter than fish grease, just furious because it was payroll's error, and they wanted me to wait two more weeks for my pay. I had returned to work from a disability leave, and they still had me on the Leave of Absence list. For eight days, CSEA Union, the union I was under, did nothing to get my money and prolonged the communication between us until April 8, 2020. The union not helping me is another story, but I'll leave that for now. They do not help *all* members, only the ones they *like*.

LOOKING FOR A PLACE ON CRAIGSLIST

During this time, I'm still looking every day for an apartment on Craigslist with my computer. I thought I was going to get this one bedroom in Signal Hill, and I filled out the application and gave a money order for thirty-five dollars for a credit check because I believed that God was going to provide a place. My credit had fallen from a 720 FICO score to 525 in just four months. Even though my credit was bad due to EDD not paying my disability claim and being half paid at my job, something kept telling me inside to keep filling out the application.

With the application, I wrote a letter explaining my situation, but the lady called me two days later and said I didn't get the place but would give me my credit check money back. I was relieved of that because I needed all my money. I looked at a room in Bellflower, and it was nice and quiet. But the lady called back the next day and said she was going to rent it to her niece. I saw a room for rent in Paramount, and it smelled like cats and dogs, and the room looked like they just made the room with some cardboard and wanted to charge rent for $600.00. I left out of there with a quickness.

My father tried to get me a room again, and I thought it would be the one in Carson again, but they wouldn't let him use his credit card over the phone and said he would have to come down again and pay. Well I didn't want my father to drive from Temple City at night because he's getting older. So we tried another place, and it was a Motel 6. It smelled like smoke and the room was all the way in the back of the building. I'm not a smoker, so I knew I couldn't stay there. I talked with the receptionist, and she gave me a "non-smoking room," but it still smelled like smoke. Plus there were homeless people hanging around, digging in the dumpster.

I didn't feel comfortable, and I wasn't going stay. My dad texted me and said, "Isn't it better than your car?"

I said, "No."

He then asked, "What are going to do?"

I quickly said, "I'm leaving and going back to LBC (Long Beach City)." He gave me a thumbs-up on the text and said, "Okay." He got an attitude because I didn't want to stay there. I found a place on Craigslist, and it was like an Airbnb. I was able to borrow money from my ex-boyfriend from tenth grade and my ex-brother-in-law. Again, I had to look up and say, "Thank you, Lord, for the blessings." I was able to afford staying there for seven days, and I rested. I had an interview during that time with the state of California for an office technician (typing) position.

My father didn't contact me for five days. When he did, I was angry and didn't respond to him. I thought to myself, *Why he would wait for five days to see if I'm okay?* I could be somewhere dead and decomposing. It hurt me terribly, but then the Lord came to my mind and said, "You can't be angry because God is your Father, and He has provided for you during this time." Ms. Joanna said the same thing to me when I told her how hurt I was. She said to me, "Stop looking for your father here, but lean and trust on your Heavenly Father, who is the creator of this earth and can do *all things*!" This lady has truly been blessed by the Lord, despite her situation. She provided the best advice, and it has stuck with me to this very day. Don't get me wrong, I still tend to want to see my father show me he cares about me or have that closeness I see other daughters have with their father's, but I get disappointed every time.

I went to look at another place, never giving up, and met an African guy who was looking at the same unit. He was good-looking, but I didn't let him know that's what I thought. He was funny because he was saying I'm beautiful, and at that time, I wasn't feeling beautiful at all. We exchanged numbers. Then I went to look at another place in Gardena. This was such a nice house, but this was for a room, and the owner of the house wanted $1,800 to move in. Yeah that's California for you, just ridiculous how outrageous it is to rent. So I'm back in my car, praying to God to give me a place to live so I can take a shower. How something so simple as a shower I used to take for granted, but not anymore.

CLOSING OF THE RESTROOMS

D aily I had to wash up in the restroom as I've said before, but one day the CDC (Center of Disease Control) said the restaurants could close their restrooms. I was so upset about that because how are customers supposed to wash their hands and, for many of us who are homeless, clean up. I was grateful that South Street and Cherry McDonald's never closed their restrooms. After a few weeks of going there, I believe they knew I was homeless, and I felt so ashamed, but I knew this was not my fault. As with other homeless people, it's not their fault. I've always said whoever works for someone or an entity, they're one or two paychecks away from homelessness if they don't get paid. I had to snap out of that feeling quickly and hold up my head and continue. During this time, I met so many homeless people and couples living in their cars, it was amazing. Some were dealing with it better than others.

DEPOSITION AND MEETING MY ATTORNEY FOR THE FIRST TIME

I had to get prepared for the deposition that was two years in the making. It's a shame I had a fall at work, and it took two years before my attorney had the deposition. I believe he was working with the defense because it shouldn't take that long for a deposition. My lawyers were making me nervous by telling me to tell the truth because the defense doesn't like me, and he wants to discredit me and put me in jail. I couldn't believe he was pressuring that point. There was no need to lie because there were witnesses to the fall, but I was still nervous.

I had never met the attorney; the original attorney passed away within a year and a half of the case. The first time meeting this attorney was at the deposition, and he said, "Don't worry, you'll be fine. Nobody is going to jail." I didn't drive because it was too far to drive to Glendale, so they called an Uber driver to pick me up. The deposition was two and a half hours, and I had a migraine. I hadn't slept well the night before because of nerves and sleeping in my car, and my shoulders were hurting. My attorney didn't care. He was too busy texting and sipping his coffee. It was finally over, and the Uber came and picked me up. The attorney went back into the attorney's office with the transcriber and defense attorney.

When I get back to my car, I sit for a while, but I knew I couldn't sleep in my car another night. I needed to rest and take a shower. I didn't want to spend any money because I knew I had to save for a room. I finally broke down and got a room at Motel 6 on PCH in Long Beach. I called one of my friends who has been homeless before, and she talked to me for about three hours. She encouraged me to keep the faith, despite what I see. I didn't sleep as good as I thought I would have, but it was nice to take a shower and wash my hair. Again, this has made me really appreciate the small things like this, which we take for granted. I saw many families living in the hotel with their children.

The next morning, I turned in my keys and asked the receptionist if they took homeless vouchers. She told me yes and whom to call. I knew about the number, which didn't help me. They only help people with children, HIV, and domestic violence victims. I'm a single woman, employed, no children, and no HIV even though I'm homeless. Nevertheless, I still put in the grind to look for a room on Craigslist. I viewed and spoke to several people. I couldn't believe some people wanted you to give them your social security number to do a credit check for a *room*! I drew the line there because I don't trust people; plus when I used to rent a room out of my two-bedroom apartment, I never did that.

ROOM FOR RENT

I t was about the second week in April; I went to see this room. It was a black couple renting the room. I felt comfortable talking to them, and the room was big enough for me. I waited two days, and the girl called me and said they would give me the room. I was really excited because I was going to have a place to live. I looked up in the sky and said, "Thank you, God." I called my father and I borrowed $800 to move in on April 16, 2020. He gave me just enough money to move in and nothing more.

I didn't have any money because I was waiting on my paycheck from the school district. I was glad I asked for $800 instead of the $750 for rent because he would have sent me just that amount, $750. The fifty dollars helped with gas and food. He called me that night, and I said, "I'm in the room now."

He said, "Okay, good." I thanked him again for the money. Even though we don't have a perfect daughter-and-father relationship, I could sense he felt a little relieved that I wasn't living in my car. He never said I had to pay him back, but I felt that he really wanted it back, so I made up in my mind when I get my money together, I would pay him back.

The stimulus check came through, and I was able to pay for my phone bill and storage after putting away my rent money. I felt uncomfortable leaving the room, and I couldn't lock my door, but they could lock their bedroom door. This bothered me for about two days, and I finally talked to the guy. He said he would have to talk to his girlfriend, but he would still need a key just in case he would have to get in the room for an emergency. I thought to myself, *This is an excuse to still be able to go into my room.* After talking to my ex-boyfriend from the tenth grade, he told me to tell him that I would pay for the damage if there was an emergency. After much praying, the girlfriend told me I could change the locks. It made me feel more at ease living there, but I really wanted my own place. I continued to look for an apartment, knowing my credit was bad. I never gave up hope that someone would give me an apartment. I just didn't know when.

GOOD NEWS COMES

I got one of the three jobs I interviewed for with the state of California on April 20, 2020, and gave my two weeks' notice to the school district on April 24, 2020. It wasn't the job I really wanted, but I said to God, "Whatever job you give me, I will take it and be grateful." I'm beginning to see that God's will be done, *not* mine! I wasn't really thinking because I was still in shock at accepting the job. The school was closed down due to the pandemic, and I couldn't work there. I could have continued being employed, receive my paychecks at the school district, and work for the state too. I would have been receiving two checks, but instead, I did the right thing and gave my two weeks resignation and returned their paycheck they sent to me on May 25, 2020. Also, I believe the district sent the check to see if I would keep it.

ISSUES WITH THE ROOMMATES

T he issues with the roommates' smoking (guy) were really getting on my nerves because I'm not a smoker and I hate the smell of smoke. It was coming through the vents, then on top of that, he wasn't working due to the pandemic. He was a hairdresser. He would keep the television up all night, well at least until 1:30 a.m., and I had to be up at 5:00 a.m. to go to work. I was so furious that I decided to fight fire with fire. I know that God doesn't want us to do what "they do in this world," but I did it anyway. So in the mornings, I made so much noise by singing and washing my face that the next night he didn't do it. It only stop for a short while, and he started again. So I spoke to him about it, and he blame turning up the television on his girlfriend's snoring.

Finally, we came to an agreement that the TV would be turned down at 10:30 p.m. Then he had to say something about me walking in the house with my shoes. He only brought this up after he received the $750 for rent. After thinking about this for a couple of days, dealing with his smoking and smoking one day that wasn't cigarettes, which made me sick, I said, "I don't care. I have to move, even if it's living in an Airbnb," which I did prior to living with them. I thought about it all, the locks on the door, smoking, TV up loud, cleaning at 11:30 p.m. with the music loud until 1:30 a.m., and walking in the house with my shoes, so the next day, I called the lady with the Airbnb. I let her know I need a place to stay around June 16, 2020. She said, "No problem. I enjoyed you staying here."

Well, my friends were telling me that I was wrong, it's his place, and I don't have a place to go to, all negative. I already had spoken to God, and I put my faith in him that He would provide. So when she said no problem, I looked up again and said, "Thank you, God!" I wanted to move out sooner, but he didn't want to give me some of my money back, saying, "I don't have problem with you. You have a problem with me." I gave him my thirty days' notice.

GOD'S MIRACLE

I looked at this place near Long Beach around May, but I didn't get it. I was crushed. It was a nice little house, had a place to park my car, and it had wood floors. I wanted wood floors because of my allergies. I had stopped thinking about this unit and was preparing myself to move in the Airbnb and put my futon, table, TV, and nightstand back into storage.

I was at home in the evening watching the civil unrest on television regarding George Floyd, and my phone rang. My voice was sort of down, and the lady said, "I don't know if you found a place yet, but it didn't work out with the other tenants. So we're offering it to you, if you're still interested."

I said yes, and my voice was up, and I had a smile on my face. I then explained to her about my credit. She said she had read everything I put down, and she still wanted to offer me the apartment. We set up a time the next day to put the security deposit down. I got off the phone and fell to my knees and started crying uncontrollably. I don't know how many times I said thank you Lord, but it was a lot. My eyes were bloodshot red from crying, but I knew this was a blessing and a miracle from God Almighty, and no one, I mean no one, had to tell me what I had just witnessed. I knew right then and there, this was my testimony to tell others soon.

MOVE-IN DAY

On June 12, 2020, it was the day I would finally move into my own apartment. We started at 7:00 a.m., and I had to drive the truck. I was nervous because I had never driven a U-Haul truck; usually the movers would drive. I said my prayer and started driving back and forth. We finished at 1:30 p.m. My place had stuff stacked so high, it was hard to move around. Nevertheless, I sat on my bed and looked around and started crying again. I was so humble that I know this homeless experience was for a reason.

I wish I never had to go through it, but it was humbling. It made me know who I and others, who believe in Jesus Christ, need to trust and lean on. I was appreciative of the things I had before, but this was a different type of humbling. This was the type that made you realize that you *didn't* do this on your *own*! God Almighty gave you a favor and a blessing. He protected me, and I never went hungry. It made me realize that you have to believe, do things toward your dreams, and have faith that they will come true, the *rest is left up to God*!

Blessings and increased faith to all who will read my testimony of God's love.

ABOUT THE AUTHOR

My name is Youlanda O. Williams. My half-sister and I were raised in a single home by my mother. I also have three half-brothers, in which we share the same father, but my sister and I have different fathers.

I grew up in the John Hay Homes projects on the Eastside of Springfield, Illinois, until I was ten years old. I moved to West Covina, California over thirty years ago which is a city in Southern California to live with my father, and it became my second home.

My work experience has been in the Special Education and Office Administration fields.

I wrote this book because the Holy Spirit convinced me to tell my story about my experience, prayers, and faith as I was living in my car. This wasn't easy because it's very hard to relieve the thirty-two days again and put it down on paper, but it was something that I felt I had to do, to help others who might be going through the same thing.

It took about a year to finally finish the book due to life, going to work, and dealing with other issues, but I'm grateful that God helped me through it. It's my testimony to His grace and unconditional love for me.

I hope you find inspiration and faith and believe that no matter what you're facing, keep pushing on and believe that God will provide because He's always on time.

CPSIA information can be obtained
at www.ICGtesting.com
Printed in the USA
BVHW081515070222
628303BV00005B/42